THE IMPACT OF ENVIRONMENTALISM:
TOWNS AND CITIES

Richard Spilsbury

www.raintreepublishers.co.uk
Visit our website to find out
more information about
Raintree books.

To order:
☎ Phone 0845 6044371
📄 Fax +44 (0) 1865 312263
✉ Email myorders@raintreepublishers.co.uk

Customers from outside the UK please telephone +44 1865 312262

Raintree is an imprint of Capstone Global Library
Limited, a company incorporated in England and
Wales having its registered office at 7 Pilgrim Street,
London, EC4V 6LB – Registered company number:
6695582

Text © Capstone Global Library Limited 2013
First published in hardback in 2013
The moral rights of the proprietor have been asserted.

Edited by Andrew Farrow, Adam Miller, and
  Diyan Leake
Designed by Victoria Allen
Picture research by Elizabeth Alexander
Illustrations by Oxford Designers & Illustrators
Originated by Capstone Global Library Ltd
Printed and bound in China by Leo Paper Products Ltd

ISBN 978 1 406 23861 7 (hardback)
16 15 14 13 12
10 9 8 7 6 5 4 3 2 1

British Library Cataloguing in Publication Data
A full catalogue record for this book is available from
the British Library.

Acknowledgements
The author and publisher are grateful to the following
for permission to reproduce copyright material:
Alamy pp. 5 (© Yadid Levy), 7 (© Kuttig - Travel - 2), 11
(© Tetra Images), 17 (© Fabienne Fossez), 24 (© Andrew
Butterton), 41 (© UKraft), 43 (© Jim Wileman), 56
(© JTB Photo Communications, Inc.); Corbis pp. 31
(© Ali Haider/epa), 49 (© Kimimasa Mayama/epa),
51 (© Handout/Reuters), 55 (Julie Dermansky);
Photolibrary pp. 15 (Das Fotoarchiv), 23 (Yang Liu/
Redlink), 32 (Mark Henley), 53 (Britain on View);
Shutterstock pp. 12 (© iofoto), 19 (© Anton Foltin), 21
(© Alex Yeung), 27 (© manfredxy), 36 (© Deymos), 39
(© Antonio V. Oquias); © Wayne Pragnell p. 45.

Cover photograph of (top) Dhobi Ghat in Mumbai,
India, reproduced with permission of Shutterstock
(© Jan S.) and (bottom) Masdar Institute of Science and
Technology, reproduced with permission of © Viktoryia
Vinnikava.

Every effort has been made to contact copyright
holders of material reproduced in this book. Any
omissions will be rectified in subsequent printings if
notice is given to the publisher.

Disclaimer
All the internet addresses (URLs) given in this book
were valid at the time of going to press. However, due
to the dynamic nature of the internet, some addresses
may have changed, or sites may have changed or
ceased to exist since publication. While the author and
publisher regret any inconvenience this may cause
readers, no responsibility for any such changes can be
accepted by either the author or the publisher.

CONTENTS

Words printed in **bold** are explained in the glossary.

CENTRES OF POPULATION

Do you live in a town or city? If so, then you are like around 3.5 billion others worldwide who live in these urban areas. Because towns and cities worldwide are centres of population, they have a huge impact on the environment. For example, all those people use many resources, create waste, and require buildings, roads, and other **infrastructure** to live, work, and get around. How have concerns about how we use and damage the environment made a difference to this impact?

Town or city?

There is no globally agreed difference between the two types of settlement, except that cities are usually bigger and recognized as more important. However, all towns and cities are urban areas, which the **United Nations (UN)** defines as having populations over 20,000.

A brief history of settlements

Urban living is quite new in human history. For much of the past, people lived in rural **settlements**, the first of which date back around 10,000 years. These were places where farmers lived together, raising crops and livestock, because resources such as water and good soil were plentiful. Settlements grew into towns and cities – or urbanized – as a result of many factors. For example, some became centres of trade, dealing in farmed goods from surrounding villages. Others urbanized because they were centres of government or religion for regions. Location is also vital in **urbanization**. For instance, Liverpool urbanized because its coastal location allowed easy sea trade between nations.

The **Industrial Revolution** in Europe and the United States in the 18th and 19th centuries saw fast urbanization. Some cities, such as Detroit or Birmingham, were located near mines where coal or iron ore were found, They grew because these resources were used to power and supply machines and factories to make goods. However, the biggest factor in urbanization in the past and today is rural workers moving into cities to find work and opportunities.

Growing settlements

Back in 1900, there were only a few cities with populations of one million or more. These included London, New York City, Paris, and Berlin. By 1950, New York City had a population of more than 10 million people, making it the world's first mega-city. Today there are over 400 cities of more than one million people and 19 mega-cities. Most of the world's mega-cities are now in Asia, the region with the highest proportion of global population. In some parts of the world, such as the east coast of the United States, there are now also megalopolises. These are groups of cities that have grown and merged into combined populations of over 40 million.

The main shopping street in Beyoglu district in the major city of Istanbul, Turkey.

Percentage of total population living in cities

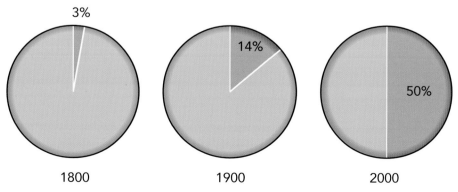

3%

14%

50%

1800

1900

2000

Urban benefits

There are many reasons why people choose to live in or move to cities, apart from work opportunities. One is good infrastructure. A city's infrastructure ranges from hospitals and universities, to airports and **public transport** systems. Another reason why people choose urban living is access to amenities. These range from libraries and colleges, to shops, swimming pools, and nightclubs. Smaller settlements generally have less extensive infrastructure, amenities, and work opportunities than bigger ones.

Urban impacts

Living in a city has impacts for individuals, for the city itself, and for our planet. The high concentration of people in cities – tens of thousands per square kilometre – can put enormous strain on, for example, water and power supply. The concentration of factories, plus the road traffic transporting workers and goods, causes atmospheric pollution in the form of poisonous gases and harmful particles. Urban air pollution kills over one million people a year.

Possibly the biggest impact is on **global warming**. You probably know the link by now – burning **fossil fuels** to release energy in vehicles and power stations also releases carbon dioxide and other **greenhouse gases**. These **emissions** remain in the atmosphere and store heat. This is making average global temperatures rise, which is causing **climate change** and increasing the frequency of extreme weather events such as heat waves or heavy storms. The 2002 UN-**Habitat** report says that the world's cities are responsible for around 70 per cent of emissions through high energy and transport use, even though they cover just 2 per cent of the total area of Earth.

Individual impact

Cities create big negative impacts, yet these result from high concentrations of people. Therefore, the impact per person is lower than in many smaller settlements. For example, the greenhouse gas emissions of an average person in the city of Denver, Colorado in the United States, with a population of just over half a million, is double that of an average New Yorker. This is largely the result of greater public transport use in New York City.

What is environmentalism?

Many of us today want to reduce our environmental impact. For example, we try to reduce our impact on the natural world and each other by turning off lights to reduce power use or recycling waste. Environmentalism is both a way of thinking and a worldwide political movement.

Environmentalism aims to protect and improve the natural environment by making changes to harmful human activities. Environmentalists range from individuals, political activists, and scientific specialists, to local and special interest groups, global charities, and other non-governmental organizations (NGOs).

What next?

In 2008, nearly three-quarters of people in **more economically developed countries** were urban, whereas under one-half were urban residents in **less economically developed countries**. By 2050, population experts predict that 70 per cent of the total global population will live in towns and cities. They predict that the fastest urbanization will continue in countries with expanding manufacturing economies and shrinking agricultural economies, such as China and India.

Cities offer a diverse range of opportunities for their large populations. This enormous indoor water park in Germany can attract many visitors each day, as it is located near the capital city of Berlin.

Growing movement

The environmentalism movement began in the 1960s and 1970s. There were many reasons for this. One was evidence of the effects of environmental pollution. For example, Rachel Carson's bestseller *Silent Spring* revealed how insecticides not only killed insects, but also concentrated in predators that ate them, harming them as well. Another was a major energy crisis in the mid-1970s, when oil and fuel costs rose in many countries. This created interest in alternative, **renewable energy** sources with less environmental impact, such as wind and solar power.

Today many countries have political Green Parties with candidates promoting changes to laws and policies that favour the environment. In many cases, the parties lobby (attempt to persuade) governments, but in Germany in the late 1990s, the Green Party shared power. The results of environmentalist pressure on governments are many. They range from the national, such as formation of the Environmental Protection Agency in the United States, to major international agreements, including the 1992 UN Earth Summit, where countries agreed to reduce carbon dioxide emissions.

Changing cities

During the Industrial Revolution, people became increasingly aware of the urban impacts of human industry. Governments made the first laws to reduce the amount of smoke pollution released from homes and factories, which was causing breathing problems and leaving dirty soot over buildings. Many towns and cities established **green spaces** with trees and gardens where workers could escape the polluted conditions where they worked. One example of an urban green space is New York City's famous Central Park.

Today urban environmentalism is not just concerned with limiting pollution and conserving urban green spaces. It also promotes saving energy and water, reducing waste and transport impacts, and making towns and cities more **sustainable**. Being sustainable involves using resources carefully so they are not depleted or permanently damaged for future generations. It not only has had a major influence on town planning and building design, but also on new technology – for instance, new designs of wind turbines for cities and low-emission cars – and new jobs, such as energy conservation officers.

Then and Now
Measuring the problem

In the 19th century, scientists were unable to measure urban pollution accurately. Up until the 1920s, they could only estimate it by sight, and by the amount of dirt on clothes or buildings. Then governments started to position deposit gauges around cities. These were graduated tubes that collected dust. Today scientists use equipment that can automatically analyse and measure the particles and chemicals in air. These machines, situated on the ground and in satellites in space, can send pollution data to computers.

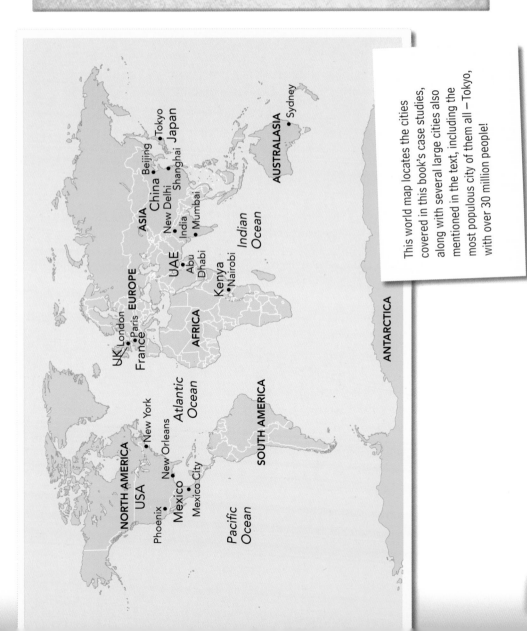

This world map locates the cities covered in this book's case studies, along with several large cities also mentioned in the text, including the most populous city of them all – Tokyo, with over 30 million people!

PLANNING AND LAND USE

Every town and city looks different in terms of the layout of buildings and roads, yet many share common features. The urban settlements we see today are usually the result of growth through time. For example, India's modern capital New Delhi has grown up around a 17th-century walled city now called Old Delhi. Some urban growth is haphazard and depends on how increasing population, industries, and amenities fit into the available space. However, parts of many towns and cities have been planned in advance.

What is planning?

In simple terms, urban planning is deciding how to develop and use land in towns and cities. The planning process involves professional planners employed by governments and councils. They identify how many people are likely to use the town or city, and how that number is likely to grow in the future. They identify what their needs are. For example, are there enough affordable houses for young people to buy, and enough schools for their children?

Apart from **residential areas** to live in, a large urban population will need office blocks, factories, and other places of work, as well as recreational areas. They will need sufficient hospitals and transport infrastructure so they can move around from work to home, and access emergency services. They need **sanitation** (the systems to supply clean water and remove dirty water) to remain healthy.

Planners work with architects, civil engineers, and builders to design cities that suit the population's needs. The layout will depend on various factors. For example, in some areas it may only be possible to create new buildings in gaps between preserved old buildings. Natural features such as hills and rivers can affect the routes roads can take. City layouts also depend on people's ideas on how they should look. For example, central Manhattan in New York has a grid layout where streets are standard distances apart, but central Paris has streets radiating around significant landmarks, such as the Arc de Triomphe.

> ### Spot the green features
> Next time you are travelling through a town or city, look for examples of environmental planning, such as industrial zones situated away from the centre.

City planners work closely with architects to design the built environments that residents, governments, and businesses need in urban locations.

Environmental planning

In the past, planners largely saw urban land as a commodity that could be bought or sold, and that should accommodate as many buildings as possible. Following the spread of environmentalism, planners now recognize urban land as having an ecological and social value that cannot be measured in financial terms. For example, most countries today have **zoning** regulations. These are laws and guidelines that state what activities can occur in different parts of the city. For example, residential zones are positioned away from the factories in **industrial zones** (which might pollute people in their homes), and shops in commercial zones, which may be very busy. Zoning also covers the size and spacing of buildings so residents are not overlooked or crammed in too closely to each other, which could affect their quality of life.

Changing plans

The work of planners is constantly changing, as people's needs change. Although planners sometimes create large settlements from scratch, they usually **redevelop** parts of existing ones. For example, in the 1960s, areas of city housing in UK cities such as London and Glasgow were knocked down and replaced with high-rise apartment blocks. The reasons for this were that the old houses were very run-down, having been constructed in Victorian times for industrial workers, and had become overcrowded owing to rising populations. Such redevelopment also modernized the cities.

Environmentalism has also had big impacts on redevelopment in cities. In recent years, planners in many cities have introduced bus and cycle lanes, and car-sharing schemes to reduce car use (see pages 34–37). Today developers in many countries are legally required to reduce construction waste and any contamination of land caused by demolition and rebuilding.

Spreading out

Growing settlements sometimes spread outwards because space is used up and land further from city centres may be cheaper. This spread is often called **urban sprawl**.

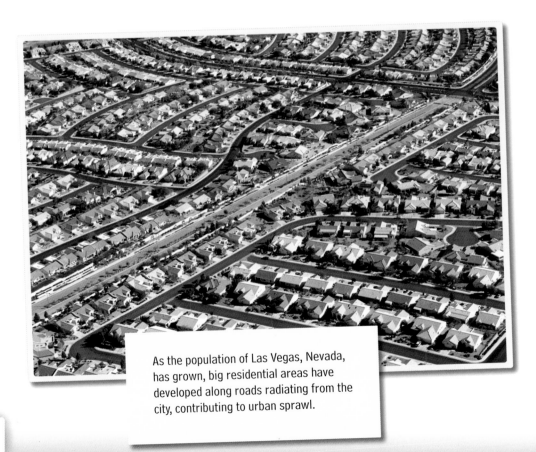

As the population of Las Vegas, Nevada, has grown, big residential areas have developed along roads radiating from the city, contributing to urban sprawl.

Many city workers move to live in housing developments in suburbs or areas outside the city. The richest may move to outlying villages or towns where they may have bigger homes and gardens. Large shopping outlets, such as malls, may also develop away from city centres.

Sprawl has environmental implications. For instance, urban workers may have to commute, making long trips to and from work each day, which results in greater vehicle emissions. In cities such as Los Angeles and Mexico City, commuting resulting from urban sprawl has caused major pollution problems, whereby exhaust fumes react with sunlight forming brown-grey, harmful **smog**. Also new suburban houses may be built on agricultural land or wild habitats.

Poor housing

The other way cities change with growing population is when **slums** develop. Slums are unplanned and densely populated areas of housing. They may develop on wasteland, or near the city industries where migrants work. Globally, around one billion people live in slums in both less and more developed countries.

Slum dwellings vary, from shacks built of sticks and plastic sheets, to substantial but run-down buildings with brick walls and tiled roofs. Sanitation conditions in many slums are appalling, so diseases spread fast. In Kibera, the largest slum in Nairobi, Kenya, **diarrhoea** is the biggest killer of young children. This is because the people there generally have to drink and wash their hands in dirty water. Slums also have poor infrastructure – for instance, the lack of schools can make literacy rates for children there much lower than for non-slum dwellers in the same cities.

What next?

In 2000, world leaders from countries in the United Nations agreed on Millennium Development Goals to improve the living conditions of 100 million slum-dwellers by 2020. However, experts predict that the total slum population will rise by five times that number by then.

ENVIRONMENTALISM IN ACTION

Dharavi slums

Location: Mumbai, Maharashtra state, western India
Settlement size: 619 square kilometres (239 square miles)
City population: 12 million

Mumbai is a one of the largest and most economically important cities in India. It is the centre of the Indian cotton, financial, and film industries. It is densely populated owing to immigration of people from the countryside to find work, and the physical limits of the island on which the city is built. Around 60 per cent of the total population lives in hundreds of slums. One of the biggest is Dharavi, where nearly one million residents live on a total area of around 3 square kilometres (1 square mile). Dharavi is famous for having appeared in the 2008 film *Slumdog Millionaire*.

Life in Dharavi

Dharavi is a maze of narrow, dirty lanes filled with crowded buildings and criss-crossed by open sewers. On average, 15 people occupy an area of 28 square metres (300 square feet). Most homes have no inside toilets, so hundreds of people may share a single public toilet, or use the nearby river. In the past, Dharavi residents generally had no running water or electricity. Today many not only have taps and power points, but also colour TVs and computers. The benefits of living there include low rents in an otherwise unaffordable city – and also jobs. Dharavi has a wide range of small-scale industries, including the production of embroidered garments and high-quality leather goods. There is no zoning in this settlement as residential, commercial, and industrial buildings are all mixed together.

Redevelopment potential

Dharavi is a developer's dream. It is right in the centre of the city, so land prices are high. It is also near several railway lines connecting it to other parts of India, so large businesses want to locate there. There have been plans to redevelop Dharavi since 2004. Some planners say the change would massively benefit slum dwellers. Families would be resettled in new high-rise blocks with indoor plumbing set amongst new shopping complexes, schools, and hospitals. Many residents are against the idea because it has been their family's home for generations – but would welcome improvements to their lives, such as better sanitation.

Reassessing Dharavi

Environmental thinking has made some urban planners see Dharavi and other slums very differently. The slum is highly sustainable. Homes use local rather than imported materials for building, and most residents walk from home to work rather than rely on polluting transport. Energy and resource use per person is the lowest in Mumbai and recycling is much higher. For example, there are 4,000 recycling units and 30,000 rag-pickers in the slum. It is also productive. Dharavi's industries annually contribute around £350 million to Mumbai's economy, but also serve the needs of the local community. This is why planners are reassessing the pros and cons of Dharavi and hoping to redevelop the slum without losing the things that make it such a productive and vibrant place to live.

A small but highly productive sewing factory in Dharavi provides low-paid but regular work close to home for residents of the slum.

Greener surroundings

People have realized the importance of green spaces in urbanized areas since at least the Industrial Revolution. As cities expanded, so they swallowed up areas of surrounding parkland on private estates, woodland, and fields. In Victorian times, towns and city planners started to introduce urban parks. These green spaces with trees and formal gardens would offer leisure facilities such as boating lakes and walkways, and a chance for urban workers to breathe clean air. Park edges also tended to be more desirable areas to live in.

Governments in some countries in the 20th century used laws to limit urban sprawl into the countryside. The United Kingdom, the Netherlands and Canada, for example, established greenbelts around some cities. These were rings of green space where farming, forestry, outdoor leisure activities, and landscape preservation would be more important than building. Today 13 per cent of the total land area of England is greenbelt.

Green spaces today

The impact of environmentalism means that today a wider range of urban green spaces is valued and conserved by both planners and city dwellers. These include wasteland and unused land along canals and railways, as well as gardens, parks, and cemeteries. Although some of these green spaces are not very attractive, they are important. For example, they provide habitats for urban wildlife and **corridors** or routes for them to move around. Green spaces also absorb the runoff of rain from city streets and concrete areas that might otherwise cause flooding. Trees are valued and preserved partly because they absorb some air pollution and improve atmospheric quality.

Planners also encourage converting green spaces such as wasteland for urban agriculture. Many cities already have allotments, or spaces where people can grow fresh food, which were set up in the past for people without space in their own gardens. However, planners have different reasons to promote urban agriculture today. Growing locally reduces the environmental impact of transporting food into cities. The insect and bird life attracted to allotment crops can also increase **biodiversity**, and food trading can stimulate local economies. In 2011, for example, San Francisco, USA, changed its zoning laws to allow farming throughout the city.

Then and Now
Seeing green

Fifty years ago, planners could often only estimate the area of green spaces. Today, planners around the world have access to high-resolution satellite images of Earth, allowing accurate measurement of city areas and green spaces. They are also able to use geographic information systems. These computer systems can output a variety of types of digital maps, allowing planners to see in a visual form the impact of population pressure, roads, and other changing infrastructure on city layout, water supply, and city amenities.

An organic market garden in central Havana, Cuba. Around one-half of the fresh vegetables, fruit, and other farmed foods eaten in the city is grown in "popular gardens" dotted through the urban neighbourhoods.

ENVIRONMENTALISM IN ACTION

Sonoran Preserve

Location: Phoenix, Arizona, USA
Settlement size: 1,095 square kilometres (423 square miles)
City population: 1 million

The desert city of Phoenix is a popular place for Americans to move to, owing to its warm climate, low land cost, cheap water, and access to national parks. This explains why its population expanded in size over three times faster than average US cities between 1990 and 2000. The growing population has caused urban sprawl northwards into the desert into an area called the North Phoenix Area (NPA). However, planners have been careful to balance needs for space with desert conservation here. This is why a new conservation area called the Sonoran Preserve was created in the NPA.

Protecting the desert

The Sonoran Desert is a harsh but beautiful habitat with a unique mixture of plants, such as giant saguaro cactuses and creosote bushes, and animals, including the poisonous gila monster lizard and burrowing owls. The habitat is under pressure not only from building and pollution, but also from activities such as gravel mining, illegal hunting, and off-road driving.

The first desert preserve, South Mountain Parkland, was established to conserve hills in the city in 1925 and subsequent preserves also protected hills from development. This was partly to provide space for hiking, horse riding, and good views. However, many of the hill preserves are isolated from the surrounding desert. In 1998, the Phoenix government approved the Sonoran Preserve Master Plan to conserve an area of especially lush desert habitat in the NPA.

From Plan to Preserve

The plan had several goals. These included preserving biodiversity, allowing natural ecological processes such as periodic flooding following heavy rains, and integrating the preserve with the city and the desert. The preserve includes corridors for wildlife to move in and out, but also encourages recreational use of the preserve for people. To achieve the goals, Phoenix agreed that the region's natural and human-built infrastructures were sufficient for 250,000 additional people. This is 100,000 more than the previously planned future population limit.

A stunning Sonoran landscape dominated by giant saguaro cacti. The challenge for Phoenix planners in further developing the Sonoran Preserve is to balance conservation with improved access for city dwellers.

The preserve today covers a third of the total 310 square kilometres (120 square miles) of the NPA. The remaining two-thirds are for current and future residential areas. Current plans include building an east-west road called the Sonoran Boulevard through the preserve. The boulevard has two lanes (rather than the originally planned six) and low speed limits. This reduces habitat impact and the risk of roadkill. Bridges along the boulevard will have tile mosaic recreations of the desert scenery to suggest an uninterrupted desert view.

"Usually roads are laid out first, then the land use is added. Whatever is left over is open space. We reversed that process."

Frederick Steiner, Arizona State University

New towns

In countries or regions with sufficient space, one solution to growing cities is to create new towns. New towns in the past, such as Welwyn Garden City near London, typically had many low-rise houses with gardens, trees along winding streets, and open spaces. They provided pleasant living conditions for commuters. Some new towns were built by industrial tycoons for their workers. These included Hershey in the United States, built from 1903 onwards by the Hershey chocolate family. Hershey contains many amenities for workers, ranging from a zoo and model railway, to a community centre containing a hospital, swimming pool, and library.

Today high sustainability is one of the most important aspects of many new towns. Homes, workspaces, and shops are positioned near each other to reduce **congestion**, vehicle pollution, and commuting. Sustainable new towns are generally small so people can walk and cycle across them. They may have a variety of energy-saving features and informal zoning laws to encourage businesses to set up. Examples of these new towns include Hammarby Sjöstad near Stockholm in Sweden, which has solar-powered street lights and systems for processing **sewage** into gas for cooking. New urban planners use modern technology to help reduce energy use and pollution, but also learn from ways of living worldwide, such as slums (see pages 14–15), to create better communities.

Transforming the old

Today urban planners in many more developed countries are carrying out a lot of urban rehabilitation. This is not just restoring old buildings in cities, but also reviving and modernizing existing sites for the current population. Generally, developers transform **brownfield** sites, which are vacant, derelict areas of land that are currently unused. Brownfield sites range from disused railway yards and docks, to abandoned factories.

Using old buildings and infrastructure can save on building materials and use far less energy than creating new areas from scratch. However, some brownfield sites are polluted from previous use in the past. These may require careful and expensive cleaning of hazardous materials to make them suitable for residential areas. In less developed countries that are keen to modernize rapidly, rehabilitation of old buildings may be less popular than in more developed countries. For example, in the run-up to the Beijing Olympics in 2008, government developers tore down old, historic housing areas where many people lived. This made space for modern stadiums and roads for the Games, as well as new commercial buildings.

Then and Now
Dock changes

From 1892 to the 1950s, Victoria Dock in Melbourne, Australia, was the city's busiest dock, exporting wool, animals, wheat, and other products. It became an industrial wasteland from the 1970s as new ports were built. In 2009, following a decade of rehabilitation, Victoria Docklands offered homes for 6,000 people, as well as a marina and restaurants. It now employs 19,000 workers and attracts 3 million visitors a year.

Cities are constantly changing. A newly demolished area of land in central London offers great potential for further urban rehabilitation.

BUILDINGS AND CONSTRUCTION

The styles of buildings and construction methods in urban settings around the globe vary dramatically. Some buildings are modern steel, glass, and concrete skyscrapers taller than any other man-made structures. Others are wood and mud constructions similar to buildings made centuries ago. The environmental movement has had an enormous influence on how new buildings are conceived, made, and fitted out.

Structure, function, and setting

A building's structure needs to suit its function. Office blocks generally need lots of space, windows for workers to see out of, and lifts and stairs for people to move around inside. Hospitals need to be much more durable and multifunctional than homes to cope with high volumes of people with different needs.

The types of material used depends very much on setting. For example, some city homes in less economically developed countries, such as the city of Dhaka in Bangladesh, may be made of locally available and cheap materials such as mud bricks and metal sheets. Those in a more economically developed and richer country, such as Norway, may be made of locally produced wood but also more costly stone or glass.

Then and Now
High buildings

The earliest skyscrapers surviving today are probably the eight-storey towers made of mud mixed with straw in the city of Shibam in Yemen 450 years ago. They are around 40 metres (120 feet) high. Today's tallest skyscraper is the Burj Khalifa in Dubai which is over 828 metres (925 feet) tall with 162 storeys. It used enough steel girders to stretch a quarter of the way around the world, and enough concrete to fill 130 Olympic swimming pools.

Chinese cities such as Shanghai are growing fast. Experts predict that between 2010 and 2025, the country will have built enough new skyscrapers to fill 10 New York-sized cities and make up one-fifth of the global construction industry.

Environmental impacts of buildings and construction

The major urban building materials in the 21st century are concrete and steel. These have significant environmental impacts. Processing and transporting these heavy materials uses lots of energy and is responsible for significant greenhouse gas emissions. For example, around 1.6 billion tonnes of cement are manufactured each year, releasing around 7 per cent of the total carbon dioxide caused by human activities. Concrete is made by mixing concrete with water and **aggregate** (sand, gravel, or rock chippings). Each year, 10–11 billion tonnes of aggregate are mined, which causes habitat destruction. In Vietnam, for example, mining limestone for cement is threatening a unique forest habitat.

Large areas of concrete in cities also have an environmental impact. Concrete absorbs a lot of heat, which creates the "heat island" effect. This is when cities become warmer than the surrounding land. One consequence is that people use more energy to keep cool with air conditioning. Also, paved and road areas do not absorb water, so heavy rains can cause flooding and high volumes of run-off in cities in some areas of the world.

Greener building materials

Architects, developers, and builders today have a wide range of greener materials available to choose from in order to make construction more sustainable. Some are made from renewable resources that are more sustainable than traditional mined materials. For example, sheep wool fleeces may be used to insulate houses rather than rock wool, which is processed from minerals. Walls can be made from stacked straw bales rather than concrete blocks or bricks.

Some renewable building materials are reused or recycled. Used tyres can be stacked and filled with soil to form the walls of houses. These are often called "earthships" as they have low impact on our planet. Greener concrete can be made by replacing some cement with waste power-station ash and using building rubble as aggregate, rather than mining fresh supplies.

Changing code

Safety is also a concern in towns and cities. Governments have established a wide range of building codes or rules about how things are built, with the aim of reducing hazards. These include installing fire doors and fire walls, and using fire-resistant materials to prevent fires spreading in and between buildings. Building inspectors monitor the building construction to make sure that builders meet the code standards.

Brighton was the first UK council to approve construction of an earthship building. The pink clay-covered walls around its edge are made from earth-filled tyres.

Then and Now
Earthquake codes

In 1995, an earthquake in Kobe, Japan, killed 6,400 people and ruined infrastructure, largely because buildings and roads collapsed. After that, the Japanese government changed the building codes. When the much bigger Tohuko earthquake struck near Tokyo in 2011, damage to buildings and roads in the city was minor.

Codes vary by location. In areas prone to earthquakes, codes may specify how buildings should be built or reinforced to withstand earthquakes. Techniques include resting buildings on rubber shock-absorbers. Green building codes ensure that buildings use less energy. The UK government code says homes should have insulation of at least 27 centimetres (about one foot) thick in the loft to prevent escape of household heat through the roof.

Globally, different green building certifications specify the features and standards that builders and homeowners should use in a building to save energy and water during use and reduce environmental impact during construction. Such certifications include Passivhaus in Germany and Leadership in Energy & Environmental Design (LEED) in the United States. Builders can apply for different LEED certificates called silver, gold, and platinum, depending on the number of green features and total energy savings. Studies suggest that achieving any LEED certificate may cost around 20–30 per cent more than a standard build initially, but a LEED building uses 20–30 per cent less energy each year and through the lifetime of the house.

Spot the green features
Look out for certificates on buildings or on machines with names such as Passivhaus, LEED, or BREEAM. These mean that they have energy-saving and other sustainable features in their design.

Using less

Today's architects and builders create buildings that can maintain urban living temperatures using less energy. They install windows with three layers of glass (called triple-glazed windows) that insulate buildings by reflecting heat back indoors, rather than letting it escape. Water can be heated by the Sun in tubes within roof-mounted panels, or by using energy produced by ground-source heat pumps, which use differences in temperature between stored heat in the ground and air temperatures. However, the direction a building faces also affects temperatures. For instance, positioning living spaces in shade reduces the need for air conditioning in warm climates.

Waste cooking oil can be recycled into a "smart" roof coating for tiles that can either absorb or reflect the Sun's heat to regulate temperatures inside a building. A natural alternative is a "living roof" planted with grasses, sedums, and other plants that will insulate and absorb water. When it is hot outside, evaporation of water cools the building.

Light and water

Light for buildings can also be provided using less energy. Light tubes are mirror-lined openings in roofs that reflect external light into a building. LED light bulbs are another low-energy option.

Fresh water is a finite resource that can be in short supply in cities (see pages 38–47). Cleaning dirty water is expensive and uses a great deal of energy. Buildings may be designed with many water-saving features. These can include gutters and tanks to harvest and store rainwater, systems to reuse **greywater** from sinks and showers to flush toilets, and even composting toilets that use little water to get rid of human waste.

Making power

Some buildings can now generate their own electricity using renewable energy rather than using power from power stations. Photovoltaic (PV) cells contain layers of materials that release electricity when sunlight strikes them. Separate panels of PV cells may be attached to roofs, facing the Sun, but cells may also be built into roof tiles.

Wind turbines can also be found in urban settings. When wind spins the turbine blades, machines called generators produce electricity. Turbines may be located on roofs or in gardens, catching horizontal gusts or updrafts caused by rising warm air in cities. They may have different designs. For example, turbines with spiral blades at ground level can spin in weak winds blowing from different directions.

Neither PV cells nor turbines work at all times of the day. However, when the systems are generating more electricity than is needed, building owners can sell the excess to power suppliers and use the money to buy power when their own systems are not generating enough for their needs.

Spot the green features
Look out for these features that are found on many sustainable buildings: solar panels, wind turbines, living roofs, triple-glazed windows, and greywater harvesting pipes and tanks.

This house has two large groups of 8 PV panels on the left of the roof and a water-heating panel on the right. The panels are mounted on the south-facing side of the roof. The house is in the United Kingdom and it receives more hours of stronger sunlight on this side than on the north.

Green industries

The demand for renewable energy technology in towns and cities has created jobs. Globally, around 2.3 million people work in renewables industries. Some of these work directly (for example, in factories making wind turbines) and others indirectly, such as for companies installing panels or making components used in the factories. Many of these industries are located in or near urban settlements and are encouraged by governments. In 2000, the German government made a law that power companies should buy electricity made using PV panels at a higher price than they normally sell electricity made in conventional power stations run on coal. Domestic demand for panels led to one-half of the world's solar power being installed in Germany by 2009.

In 2011, the biggest global wind and solar industries were in China. The country has ambitious plans to produce 15 per cent of its energy renewably by 2020. But in 2011, most renewable products made in China were exported, mostly because the cost of installing them is too high for the majority of Chinese people. However, this is likely to change as renewable technology gets cheaper and domestic demand rises.

Inequalities

There are many building and construction differences between less and more economically developed countries. In less economically developed countries, there may be poorly monitored building codes and dangerous building materials for sale. For example, asbestos is widely used as a cheap, durable, and fireproof material for roofing and water pipes in countries including India and Brazil, yet it is banned in 50 more economically developed countries because exposure to asbestos is linked to cancer.

One solution for creating low-cost sustainable housing in less economically developed countries is to use local green building materials. For example, metal sheeting is widely used as cheap roofing, yet this provides no insulation against heat or cold and is noisy when it rains. Agricultural waste such as straw can be mixed with locally available **resin** to make cheap sheets that insulate the metal. Ash made by heating rice husks can also be mixed with lime and water to make an alternative to concrete. Around 120 million tonnes of this rice waste are available annually in rice-growing countries such as China and Thailand.

Solar power

Some scientists believe that solar power stations will produce a quarter of the world's electricity by 2050. Solar power stations are either large installations of PV panels linked together, or groups of mirrors. These generally reflect and concentrate the Sun's heat onto fluids in tubes. The high temperatures heat water into steam that is used to generate power. In 2011, the solar PV industry employed around 170,000 people. Experts predict that by 2030, the industry could employ over 6 million people making solar power stations or solar technology for homes and other buildings.

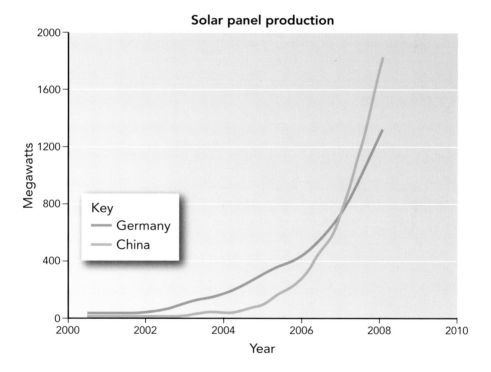

Solar panel production

Key
— Germany
— China

This graph shows how government encouragement for solar power increased production of solar panels in Germany from around 2000 onwards. Production in China rose faster, yet there are far fewer panels installed there than in Germany. This is because most Chinese panels were made to sell abroad cheaply in countries such as Germany!

ENVIRONMENTALISM IN ACTION

Masdar City

Location: Abu Dhabi, United Arab Emirates
Settlement size: 6 square kilometres (2.3 square miles)
City population: estimated 50,000

In 2008, developers started to construct a brand new city near Abu Dhabi City, capital of the United Arab Emirates, on the edge of the Persian Gulf. Masdar City is planned as one of the world's most sustainable cities completely powered by renewable energy.

Inside Masdar

Masdar City was planned to resemble traditional desert cities. It will have closely positioned buildings that provide shade and channel cooling breezes through gaps so that less energy needs to be used on cooling systems. The city will also use modern techniques. During the hottest part of the day, roof-mounted solar panels will extend and shield public spaces in the city. Most electricity will come from a solar power plant on the outskirts of the town.

Masdar City is small enough to walk around, but citizens will be able to use electric cars, buses, and also an underground transport system. It is expected that 40,000 commuters will eventually come into the city to work in its industries. Drinking water for the city will be seawater that has been desalinated using the Sun's heat. Wastewater from buildings will be reused to irrigate trees and other plants in the city.

Why create Masdar?

Abu Dhabi grew into a prosperous country after the discovery of large oil reserves in the 1950s. It still produces a lot of oil. However, global oil supplies are running out and fossil fuels will not be able to meet energy demand in the long-term future. Abu Dhabi is planning Masdar City as a showcase for renewable technology and sustainability solutions that will kick-start new industries. The city has a graduate university to research future green technologies and encourage renewable manufacturing industries. Thus Masdar will help Abu Dhabi develop a range of expertise, not simply grow its economy. In a few decades, the Abu Dhabi government hopes its economy will rely less on oil and more on renewables. It is investing around £2 billion in the city, but Masdar could generate £4.8 billion annually through new industries.

Downsides

Abu Dhabi has not always been so environmentally friendly. The average Abu Dhabi citizen has one of the highest **carbon footprints** on Earth, largely because they use a lot of cheap oil in their huge vehicles, and a great deal of electricity for air conditioning. There are many resource-wasting attractions in the country, such as golf courses in the desert and indoor skiing facilities. Critics of Masdar say that rather than spending so much money on such a tiny settlement, Abu Dhabi could invest in using less energy throughout the country, which would benefit the environment even more.

> "From the beginning, Masdar has been engaged in a journey of discovery to create a blueprint for the future of sustainable cities."
>
> Sultan Al Jaber, CEO of Masdar

Wind towers have long been used in hot desert settlements to channel hot air from ground level upwards and also to create cooling air movements. This new version in Masdar Institute, Masdar City, also has adjustable gaps on all sides at the top to capture wind and direct it downwards, helping to make life at street level much more comfortable.

URBAN TRANSPORT

Urban transport has had major impacts on urban living. These range from air pollution and congestion to increased mobility and new city layouts. The environmental movement has focused attention on the downsides of rising urban traffic and stimulated big changes in urban transport.

Changing city traffic

The growing concentrations of people in cities in the 19th century spurred inventors to come up with transport solutions for the public. The first public transport systems included horse-drawn buses in France and steam cable cars in US cities such as San Francisco. Local steam and electric trains and electric trams started to appear in many cities, and the first underground railway was built in the late 19th century in Berlin. City developers started to widen streets to accommodate more trams and the first cars.

Throughout the 20th century, cities became increasingly dominated by road transport – partly because it offered flexible routes compared with fixed rail transport. Cars also became cheap enough for more people to buy. In the second half of the 20th century, cities started to become congested with cars, buses, and lorries. Flyovers, ring roads, islands, and dual carriageways were built in and around cities to ease the flow of vehicle traffic in and out or past cities.

Rush hour traffic in Beijing. Car ownership is growing so fast in China that by 2030 there could be more cars in that one country than there were in the whole world in 2000!

Traffic impacts

Traffic in cities causes significant air pollution worldwide. Vehicle engines that burn oil-based fuels release poisonous gases and tiny soot and dirt particles (see the table below). These irritate people's throats, eyes, and lungs, and can trigger anything from asthma attacks to premature death. Levels of pollution in cities vary widely as a result of several factors. In less economically developed countries, there may be a higher proportion of older, more polluting vehicles on the roads than in more economically developed countries. Pollution also depends on traffic flow. Engines pollute more on congested roads, where vehicles frequently stop and start, than on roads where traffic is flowing more freely. The pollution impact is especially high for people living within 150–500 metres (500–1,500 feet) of traffic hotspots in cities.

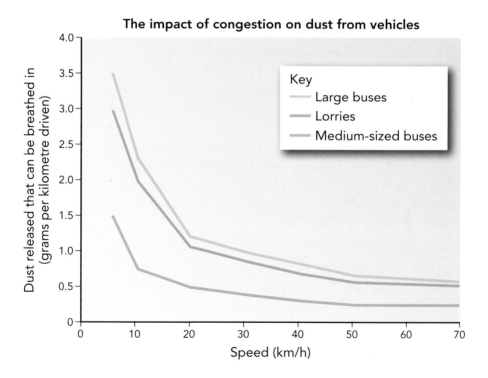

The impact of congestion on dust from vehicles

Key
— Large buses
— Lorries
— Medium-sized buses

There are other impacts on health caused by the growing dependence on urban road transport. One is that urban dwellers exercise less. The World Health Organization says that 3.2 million people die annually as a result of heart disease, cancer, and diabetes linked with physical inactivity. In addition, the increase of road traffic is causing more accidents. Over one million people die on roads each year, many in towns and cities.

Limiting traffic

The growing numbers of vehicles is putting huge pressure on the transport infrastructure in many cities. Urban planners and governments can lessen the environmental and human impacts of traffic by limiting the volume. They may pedestrianize central urban shopping areas to exclude vehicles. They may raise taxes or introduce congestion charges, whereby people have to pay to drive into city centres. In some cities, such as Bogotá (Colombia), there are no-drive days and control over which vehicles can use roads on different days. Many cities have car pooling schemes so fewer urban cars are used more frequently by more people. In some such schemes, people share lifts to and from work; in others, people hire cars for short periods.

Transport options

Limiting traffic can sometimes have a negative impact on trade. In larger cities, however, there is often public transport for shoppers and workers to use to get around, including subways, trams, and city buses. Public transport allows large numbers of people to move around cities relatively fast. The environmental movement has made people aware of the sustainability of public transport. Buses or trains generally produce more emissions than cars, but because public transport carries more people, each passenger has less environmental impact. Public transport also reduces congestion and air pollution, both of which have economic costs. This is why, for example, the city of Delhi in India invested in an expensive new underground train system in 1998.

Modern trains and buses are increasingly sustainable as a result of technological changes. For example, urban buses in cities such as São Paulo in Brazil and Munich in Germany have hybrid engines. These run partly on diesel, and partly on electricity from a motor that uses energy released during braking. Such engines consume a third less fuel and produce lower greenhouse emissions than purely diesel engines.

Then and Now
Road users

From the beginning of the 20th century to the present day, the number of passenger vehicles has increased from just a few thousand to around 1.2 billion worldwide. Population experts look at rates of car manufacture and changes in income and economies to predict how car use will change in future. They predict that by 2050, the number of cars on the road could double, and mostly in urban areas of less developed countries.

Low-emission cars

Many of the cars we see in cities today (for instance, Smart Cars) are small, light, easy to park, and have high fuel efficiency. Some cars have hybrid engines or are fully electric. But the batteries for electric cars need to be charged up using electricity often produced by fossil fuels. In some cities, you might see hydrogen cars. These have special batteries that run on liquid hydrogen, which can be made using seawater and solar power, and emit only water vapour.

More sustainable urban transport solutions are in growing demand and are often encouraged by governments. This not only lowers the carbon footprint of cities but also creates many job opportunities for designers and engineers, car dealers, and public transport networks.

Smart roads

Designers have created green technology to help limit urban congestion. For example, sensors on street lamps and in roads monitor the movement of vehicles on congested routes and send data to computers. These update display panels showing how long urban journeys will take. Drivers can then choose alternative routes or decide to use public transport. These could be widespread on urban routes in future.

ENVIRONMENTALISM IN ACTION

London bikes

Location: London, UK
Settlement size: 1,706 square kilometres (659 square miles)
City population: 7.5 million

In 2010, a new transport feature appeared in central London – blue bike hire stations and bikes for public use. This was part of a plan to increase cycling in the city four-fold between 2000 and 2025, and thereby help reduce energy use in urban transport.

Public transport in London

Each morning, around three-quarters of the one million people who travel into central London arrive by rail. Rail and bus are the dominant public transport in the city. The local government department Transport for London integrates rail, underground, bus, and boat transport networks. In 2008, Ken Livingstone, the London mayor at the time, announced initiatives to add cycling to this network, to improve both transport sustainability and the health of citizens.

By sponsoring the blue bikes in London, Barclays gets widespread advertising and positive publicity linking their brand with sustainable living. The scheme is good for businesses, people, and the environment.

Changing London for cyclists

The initiatives changed the infrastructure for cyclists. Cycle routes and cycle boxes at traffic lights were marked out to give more traffic priority to bike users. For example, some important cycle routes from outer to inner London were marked out in blue tarmac as Cycle Superhighways to enable safe and fast bike commuting. In addition, extra cycle parking was installed at train and tube stations. The final initiative was a major cycle hire scheme costing £140 million, sponsored by Barclays Bank. London modelled its cycle initiative on the successful hire schemes called Bixi in Montreal, Canada, and Velib in Paris, France.

London cycle hire

The cycle hire scheme is a new network of 6,000 identical bikes at 400 docking stations citywide. Riders pay online or by phone for a keycode to use for a set period of time. For example, it costs £1 for 24 hours. They use the keycode to unlock a bike. It is free to ride a bike for the first half-hour, but prices rise for long trips to encourage people to return bikes quickly for the next person to use. A variety of cycle routes are available for different users, from quick commuter trips to tourist routes incorporating quiet canal paths or historic sights. The cycles have baskets, mud guards, reflectors, and lights that come on automatically when riding, for safety.

Slow start

In the first three months, there were 1.4 million journeys from docking stations. Only a small percentage of these raised money to help pay back the cost of setting up the scheme, because most rides were less than 30 minutes (these short hires are free under the scheme). There were also problems for some users. Sometimes there were not enough bikes to hire at busy places such as railway stations. Docking stations that were full up forced users to spend time and money cycling around to find an alternative. The plan to repay costs within three years looked impossible. However, by November 2010 there were seven times more trips each month than at the start of the scheme.

In 2011, there were further initiatives to encourage more cycling in London. These included the Mayor of London's annual Sky Ride in Central London, where road traffic is banned from central streets for a day so cyclists can rule the roads.

"We want nothing short of a cycling transformation in London."
Ken Livingstone, Mayor of London, 2008

WATER AND WASTE

The high concentration of people living in and using towns and cities puts great pressure on water resources and creates large volumes of industrial and domestic waste. The environmental impacts of supplying water and waste are stimulating changes in resource use in towns and cities worldwide.

Water in cities

Cities use a lot of water. For example, Mexico City's 20 million citizens use 15 million cubic metres of water daily – enough to fill 6,000 Olympic-sized swimming pools! City factories use water to cool machinery, or to make products such as food or concrete. Homes and businesses use water for cooking, washing, flushing toilets, and gardens.

Water demands in many cities, especially in less economically developed countries, are also high because of inadequate water-supply infrastructure. Over 40 per cent of all freshwater is lost through leaking pipes in large Asian cities. Supplying water can create other problems in cities. For example, most of Mexico City's water is extracted from spaces in rocks beneath the city. This is causing rocks to collapse and buildings to subside.

However, 1 in 8 people around the world do not have access to safe, treated water to drink, through either private or public taps. Urban dwellers in less developed countries may only have access to water from polluted city rivers. One of the biggest sources of pollution is human sewage. This contains harmful bacteria that causes diarrhoea and diseases such as cholera – both major killers. Ninety per cent of cities in less developed countries release untreated human sewage from toilets straight into rivers, lakes, and seas. In urban slums, most people have no toilets, and "flying toilet" (defecating into plastic bags and throwing them on the ground or into rivers) is common.

Urban waste

Towns and cities produce vast quantities of waste, ranging from lawn clippings and uneaten food, to plastic packaging, batteries, and obsolete computers. In more developed countries, there may be regular waste collection services organized by governments, but in less developed countries, waste may pile up on streets. Three-quarters of the world's waste is dumped in **landfill sites**. These are holes in the ground where the rubbish slowly rots down. The liquid released seeps from landfill sites, polluting soil and water in cities.

Some urban waste is burnt in **incinerators** instead of being dumped. Although this may be a useful source of energy, polluting chemicals in smoke from incinerators can cause breathing problems.

The remaining waste urban dwellers produce is recycled. In more economically developed countries, recycling of steel tins, aluminium drinks cans, and paper is widespread. However, in less developed countries, a much wider range of waste, including many types of plastic and electrical goods, is recycled. Around 10 million very poor people rely on waste-picking on streets or dumps for their day-to-day survival.

People crowd around a newly arrived rubbish truck at a landfill site in Cavita, the Philippines, in the search for valuable recyclable items in the waste.

Conserving water supplies

Central to the environmental movement is understanding how human activities influence natural ecosystems and water supplies. For example, forests are important for holding on to soil and trapping water. Tree roots and soil can also clean pollutants from water as part of a natural process. When people cut down forests, water quality drops – and it costs more to clean water for our use. One study worked out that the economic value of water storage in China's forests is around $1 trillion. Many cities, ranging from Seattle, USA, to Manila in the Philippines, protect nearby forests from deforestation to maintain good water supply.

Water availability in cities can increase if each person uses less – for example, by using a shower rather than taking a bath, replacing old toilets with new ones that use less water, and mending dripping taps. Smart water meters can show how much water is used at different times for different activities. A study in California found that people with smart meters used 17 per cent less water than those with ordinary meters. Many experts say that making people pay more for water is the best way to encourage lower use. In Mexico City, an increase in water charges led to citizens installing hundreds of thousands of reduced-water flush toilets and 28 billion litres (20.6 billion gallons) less water being used each year – enough to fill 31,200 Olympic-sized swimming pools.

Sourcing water

Another way to reduce our use of treated, mains water in cities is to harvest more untreated rainwater from roofs of buildings, and to reuse greywater. Greywater can come from a variety of sources. When it is filtered, it is clean enough for use in washing machines or for watering gardens. Water used once by industries such as steel makers in cities can be reused many times. Solutions to problems of water pollution in less economically developed countries include improving water infrastructure – from more taps to more water treatment plants – and making river water safer to drink at a low cost. An example of this is the lifestraw – a special straw with filters that remove all bacteria and other tiny organisms that cause diarrhoea. People can use a lifestraw to drink safe and clean water even from dirty rivers.

Spot the green features

Look out for the following water saving features: twin flush buttons on domestic toilets, or signs showing that public toilets use less water.

Water roles

Today there is a whole range of new urban jobs and industries concerned with sustainable water use that did not exist before the environmental movement. Some companies design and manufacture greywater harvesting systems, from pipes, pumps, and storetanks to channel and collect the water, to special filters and water-purifying equipment for cleaning water prior to use. Other companies regulate water use in cities. For example, UK-based Pureworld assesses water footprints, which are a measure of how much water an organization is using and wasting. They inspect student living quarters, for instance, to check for leaks and water quality.

DaimlerChrysler car company in Berlin harvests rainwater from its building roofs, which cover an area of 32,000 square metres (344,000 square feet) – the same area as eight football pitches. The large radiating gutters seen here take the water to a large underground tank used, for example, to flush the company's toilets.

Reducing and reusing

Environmental solutions to the waste problem in cities can be broadly divided into the three Rs: Reduce, Reuse, and Recycle. Reducing waste involves making choices about what we buy or use. For example, parents may choose reusable, washable nappies rather than disposable nappies. Disposables use more energy and resources to produce, and generate 60 times more solid waste in landfill sites. Washing nappies can create polluted water, but the environmental impact is much lower. Reusing items to reduce waste can involve anything from patching holes in bike tyres, refilling shower gel bottles, or donating old mobiles to charities that refurbish them for use in poorer countries.

Recycling more

Recycling more also reduces waste. This involves consumers separating waste into different types such as paper, metal, plastic, glass, and organic waste. Organic waste includes garden cuttings and vegetable peelings. This waste is naturally **decomposed** or rotted by bacteria, forming compost that can be used to improve garden soil. Many urban councils encourage home composting of organic waste – partly for use on the garden, but mostly to reduce decomposition in landfill sites. Decomposition releases **methane** gas that stores more heat per molecule than carbon dioxide in the atmosphere, so contributing more to climate change.

Managing waste

Sustainable waste management in towns and cities requires good infrastructure for waste handling. This involves not only collection vehicles and recycling facilities where waste can be separated, but also businesses and organization networks that can deal with waste and its impacts. These include specialist workers, such as metal recyclers, and waste managers in businesses and at landfill sites.

The most sustainable landfill sites are lined with concrete to prevent pollution seeping into the soil. They have teams of diggers to bury waste so it does not attract flies and birds that could spread bacteria. They also have pipes to collect methane. This gas can be used to provide fuel for heating. Urban power stations can use methane to create electricity. These processes are often called **waste-to-energy**. Landfill site managers organize recycling of materials where possible and charge people or businesses more to dispose of environmentally harmful materials, such as asbestos or oil.

Then and Now
In the bin

In 1892, the largest proportion of household waste in the United Kingdom was dust and cinders from open fires that burned coal and wood. In those days, "dustmen" made a living picking through waste to recover coal dust they could make into fuel. There was virtually no organic waste. In 2011, garden and kitchen organic waste make up around one-half of the total percentage of household waste – and plastic waste (which did not exist before the mid-20th century) makes up around 10 per cent.

In 2007, Modbury became the first UK town to become a plastic-bag-free zone – no business gives out standard non-biodegradable plastic carrier bags. However, customers who have forgotten their own bag to take their goods home can buy one made of corn starch, which they can put in the recycling bin after use.

Spot the green features
Look out for: recycling centres, green and brown wheelie bins, composting bins, and reuseable shopping bags for sale.

ENVIRONMENTALISM IN ACTION

Sustainable Sydney 2030

Location: Sydney, Australia
Settlement size: 12,406 square kilometres (4,790 square miles)
City population: 4.1 million

Sustainable Sydney 2030 is an ambitious programme and vision for an improved city. Central to this are plans to rethink how water and waste are used and disposed of in the city. Part of the programme is a major campaign called Zero Waste to reduce the amount of waste going to landfill sites.

How the programme developed

Sustainable Sydney began as part of Australia's national policy of reducing greenhouse gas emissions. It grew into a bold vision of a future city. The city government worked out the programme over 18 months by consulting 12,000 people, and using thousands of comments, most of which were posted on its 2030 website. The people wanted a future Sydney to be: Green, Global, and Connected.

"Global and Connected" refers to improvements in international and local business, tourism, and cultural links. People wanted to live in a city where they feel at home, are connected to the local community and wider world, and that encourages art and culture. "Green" incorporates plans for a new green infrastructure to reduce energy, water, and waste demands. It was a clear message that, in Sydney, the environment matters.

Cutting water use

A central part of Sydney's plan is to harvest more rainwater for urban use. At present, only one-tenth of treated, drinking-quality water from a major reservoir near Sydney is actually used for cooking and drinking. The rest is used for toilets and air conditioners. The city is planning a recycled water network across the city to harvest and distribute rainwater. This will be used to replace drinking-quality water for flushing toilets, in fire hoses, and to irrigate sports fields, for example. Harvesting sites include sports centres, police stations, and kindergartens. The council has also mended leaks in water pipes, and put low water-use fittings in parks and community facilities. These measures have reduced the use of drinkable water by 17 per cent.

Rain gardens

When it rains heavily in Sydney, oil, waste, and soil wash from lawns, gardens, drives, urban streets, and squares into storm drains which then run directly into the harbour or into Cooks River. Part of Sydney's green water plan is to prevent urban run-off – both to save water and to reduce pollution.

The city is achieving this partly by creating "rain gardens" alongside paths, roads, and open spaces. These are sunken, decorative flowerbeds containing deep-rooted native plants. The beds have layers of stones and soil to slow down and retain storm water, and the plant roots clean pollutants from the water. Gradual evaporation of water from the rain gardens also helps cool the city during hot spells.

These are views of a rain garden beside a busy street in Sydney.

"This ... will enable us to retrofit the City with green technologies and infrastructure ... – from wires and pipes, to solar panels, water recovery, and waste treatment facilities – efficiently, cost effectively, and sustainably."
Clover Moore, Mayor of Sydney, 2010

Improving waste treatment

The average Sydney household sends around half a tonne of waste to landfill each year, but the city has a target to recycle around 70 per cent. The city opened its first alternative waste treatment (AWT) facility at Kemp's Creek in 2009, and a second in 2011 at Jack's Gully. Both are able to recover a wide range of recyclable materials from household waste. Some organic waste at the AWTs is composted, but some goes into anaerobic digesters. These are special tanks where chopped organic waste decomposes faster than in landfill sites, creating methane fuel. Using this methane reduces the amount of gas entering the atmosphere, and also reduces how much fossil-fuel gas needs to be bought. Waste-to-energy reduces landfill and helps reduce the city's carbon footprint by 3 per cent.

Changing attitudes to landfill

The extra cost of setting up infrastructure and employing people at AWTs is about twice per tonne of waste than tipping it into landfill sites. However, the Sydney government is encouraging people to deal with waste more responsibly in different ways. It is using laws to charge waste collectors more to dump in city-run landfill sites. This makes dumping less cost-effective.

Sydney's Zero Waste campaign is making consumers deal with their waste. For example, the city designates special days when people can take electronic waste, or **e-waste** such as batteries and mobile phones to AWTs with the pledge that 95 per cent of this will be recovered and reused. It educates people about the environmental hazards of e-waste in terms of the toxic chemicals it contains.

The city also supports a national scheme for managing e-waste, which encourages the companies who make electronic products to accept lifetime responsibility for their goods. This means they would be responsible for recycling products at the end of their useful life. Such measures could encourage companies to create less waste and make longer-lasting products that can be upgraded rather than dumped.

"The most critical decision that local governments make about greenhouse gas reduction is what they do with their waste, which can account for twice the emissions profile of their motor vehicle fleet."

Eric Gernath, Managing Director, SITA Environmental Solutions

New waste technology

Sydney relies on a fleet of over 30 vehicles to collect waste each week from thousands of bins. This includes around 800 tonnes of rubbish, some of which can be recycled. There are several problems with waste collection. Waste vehicles use fuel and create emissions, and waste bins smell and may attract pests. Part of Sydney's vision of the future is to install an underground vacuum system on city streets linked to buildings. The idea is that people put waste directly into the system. It would then be sucked at speeds of around 70 kilometres (40 miles) per hour to a waste station. A computer system would use sensors to identify different types of waste and separate them into garbage and items for recycling.

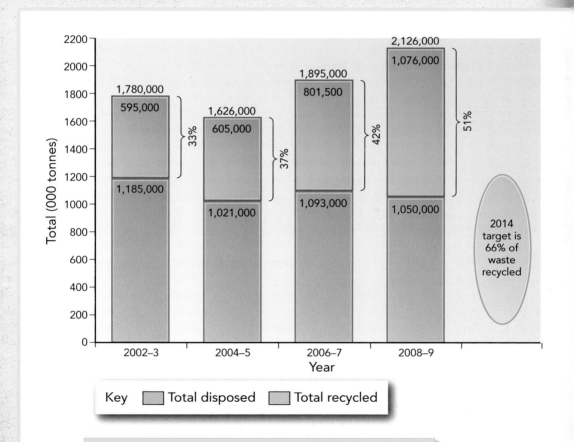

This bar chart shows how the proportion of waste that is recycled from Sydney's total waste has been rising through the first decade of the 21st century. It is hoped that the 2014 target for recycling of 66 per cent will help to slow or decrease the volume of waste going to landfill.

THE URBAN COAST

Coasts are popular places to live, and most of the largest cities on Earth are near or next to the sea. The ocean brings benefits to the urban coast but these settlements are also vulnerable to its changing environmental impacts.

Coastal cities

Cities first developed along coasts where they served the fishing industry and ocean trade. In more recent times, coastal cities have become important places for immigrants to arrive in countries, for goods to be manufactured for export, and for tourists attracted by their blend of culture, economic development, and scenery. About two in every five people on Earth live within 100 kilometres (60 miles) of coasts, and populations of coastal cities are rising fast. Two-thirds of those cities projected to have a population of eight million or more by 2015 are coastal.

Climate change and sea level

Human use of fossil fuels is widely accepted to be causing global warming. Higher temperatures are causing gradual **sea-level rise**. This is happening for two main reasons. One is that warmer temperatures cause water in oceans to expand so that it takes up a greater volume. The other is that warmer atmospheric temperatures are melting glaciers and sea ice, especially in the Arctic and Antarctic regions. Scientific records reveal that a change of around 15 centimetres (6 inches) occurred during the 20th century.

Sea-level rise would flood some coastal cities with seawater causing damage to property and disruption to transport and businesses. For example, a 1-metre-high rise in New York City would flood the subway system unless preventative measures were taken. Sea-level rise could also prevent sewage outflow to the sea, causing greater pollution in cities. Saltwater and sewage may contaminate freshwater supplies.

Vulnerable cities

Global warming is causing changes to weather patterns in many places. These events normally cause coastal damage through high winds and **storm surge**, which is when high waves created by the winds wash on to land. In coastal cities, sea-level rise will increase the effects of storm surge. The catastrophic tsunami wave produced by the 2011 Tohoku earthquake off Japan demonstrated the effects of seawater rushing on to large areas of land. Apart from over 18,000 people losing their lives, nuclear reactors were damaged and airports were flooded.

The power of the ocean wiped out coastal communities in Japan after the 2011 tsunami, and left rubble strewn across the land.

Sea level

Scientists predict that the level of greenhouse gas emissions in the past and future will cause rises in sea level of between 18 and 79 centimetres (7 and 32 inches) by 2100. The exact amount depends on many factors. Higher temperatures could increase snowfall at the poles, so less water goes into oceans. Snow and ice normally reflect heat back into space. However, when this melts, the exposed darker seawater and land absorb more heat and melt ice faster. Also, warming glaciers could slide faster into the sea and therefore melt faster than their current rates.

Direct coastal impacts

Half of the world's coasts are threatened by development. Creating or enlarging towns and cities on coasts has many direct impacts on the environment, such as destroying natural habitats. Developers clear natural coastal habitats, such as seagrass beds and mangrove vegetation, to create land for building. Between 1980 and 2005, an area of mangrove the size of Belgium was removed globally.

Mangrove swamp habitats are important safe havens for young fish that will eventually grow into the fish stocks that the coastal fishing industries rely on. They form natural barriers to storm surges, and thus protect settlements. They can also absorb carbon dioxide from the atmosphere more efficiently than forest trees. Removing mangrove can have a negative impact on the global warming problem.

Soil and sand exposed to waves and wind wash into the sea, and may cover and kill coral reefs that need sunlight to survive. Creating ports, docks, and seafronts uses enormous amounts of concrete. In some coastal settlements, much of the aggregate used in concrete is dredged from the sea floor. This causes direct environmental damage, but changing the level of the seafloor also impacts on wave patterns and the shape of beaches, which is important to coastal tourism.

Working with the sea

Governments and developers in cities need to take action to defend their buildings, infrastructure, and people against the rising oceans. This is partly because it is very expensive to deal with emergencies and repairs caused by coastal flooding. Between 2000 and 2010, UK insurance companies paid out over £4 billion repairing flood water damage. By 2035, it could cost this amount each year!

One option for dealing with the problem is to move settlements inland further from land worst affected by flooding. Retreat is usually impractical, especially for larger cities (owing to size) and those in less developed countries, where cost is an issue. However, in some cities, such as Ventura in California, USA, people have moved sections of urban development such as roads and car parks further from the sea to escape damage.

Changing the level of the sea floor has other impacts. Removing material deepens the sea floor, allowing larger waves to hit shore, which in turn results in more erosion. This can increase the loss of sand on beaches used by wildlife – for example, where turtles usually lay eggs – and by tourists. Many coastal settlements rely on the tourism industry for part of their income.

Recovering wetlands

In some urban areas, people are restoring natural habitats that help prevent urban flooding. For example, in the mid-1990s, the Chinese government decided that the growing city of Shanghai needed a new airport. Engineers drained wetlands 30 kilometres (19 miles) from Shanghai to create land for Pudong International Airport. However, the new land was at risk of flooding from storm surges caused by typhoons hitting the east coast of China.

Part of the solution was for engineers to create new wetlands on natural sand banks in the Yangtze River estuary. They carved new channels and planted large areas of seagrasses to stabilize the land. The wetland will help to keep floodwaters from Pudong and Shanghai and also increase air safety. This is because it provides habitat for water birds such as geese and gulls that might otherwise stay near the airport and fly into aeroplane engines.

This aerial view of the resort city of Cancún, Yucatán, Mexico, shows coastal development in progress on land cleared of mangrove. The coral reefs off the shore of Cancún are gradually being destroyed partly by algae cloaking their surface. The algae grow fast in these warm waters owing to large amounts of nutrients in treated sewage run-off from Cancún.

Defence

A second option to prevent flooding is defence. In some cities, such as St Petersburg in Russia, governments have built flood barriers. These gated bridges use machines to hold back approaching water along rivers from the sea. They are very expensive – St Petersburg's cost nearly £2 billion – but cheaper than paying for major flood damage.

Some coastal settlements use thick sea walls or gabions (rocks held in place by steel cages) to hold back the sea. In others, such as New Orleans, governments have constructed raised ridges called dikes, or **levees**, as a barrier to the sea. They then use pumps to remove any floodwater that gets in. Half of the land area of low-lying Netherlands is reclaimed from the sea. One of its newest cities, Lelystad, was created in 1967 when Dutch engineers drained water from an inland sea.

City planners are also preparing for higher coastal water levels in future. For example, in Melbourne, Australia, the new Victoria Docklands development (see page 21) stipulates that the lowest level of a building in regular use by people should be 2.2 metres (7 feet) above sea level. Only car parks and services should be built below this level.

Attack

The final tactic in flood defence is to redevelop cities by building out on to the water. This approach adapts to changes in sea levels and extreme weather affecting coasts. For example, in places such as Maasbommel in the Netherlands, architects have developed floating homes. These rest on slabs of concrete-coated foam and have flexible mooring posts sunk into the seafloor so they can rise with the water. In future, airports and whole neighbourhoods might float.

In the waters off Abu Dhabi and Dubai, engineers have created artificial islands, raised well above sea level in anticipation of sea-level rise. Engineers sink metal supports into the seafloor, build up rocks, and then top with millions of tonnes of sand, dredged from the sea floor or moved from inland dunes. A British study in 2010 suggested a cheaper way of creating islands in future, by reusing enormous oil rigs no longer in operation. The rigs would be linked to the mainland by bridges and to each other by walkways. Some could be residential and others entertainment complexes. To be sustainable, power would be generated using the force of the tides beneath the rigs.

Then and Now
Flooding in Netherlands

In the past, the Dutch used windmills to pump water from land. In spring 1953, a storm surge pushed seawater up to 5.6 metres (18.4 feet) higher than sea level into the Netherlands, causing major flood damage and killing hundreds of people. The Dutch government then defended their country from floods by using barriers to the North Sea including the 3-kilometre- (1.5-mile-) long Oosterschelde storm-surge barrier, completed in 1986. Since that time, the barrier has had to close its gates 24 times to protect the country from storm surge.

The cylinder shapes in the centre of the Thames flood barrier, London, are rotating gates linking the concrete piers. When high tides or storm surge threaten London with flooding, powerful engines in the tall silver structures raise the gates using the yellow arms. This then prevents the movement of water between the piers.

Integrated water management

Location: New Orleans, Louisiana, USA

Settlement size: 516 square kilometres (199 square miles)

City population: 239,000

In August 2005, Hurricane Katrina, one of the deadliest hurricanes in US history, caused catastrophic flooding in New Orleans after flood defences failed. As a result, the city's government is taking a new, more sustainable, integrated approach to preparing for and coping with future floods.

Flood control

New Orleans, one of the oldest cities in the United States, was first built on swampy land near the Mississippi River and Lake Pontchartrain as a trading centre. Draining the swamplands over time has resulted in a city that lies as low as 3 metres (10 feet) below sea level. From the early 19th century onwards, US government engineers have built 560 kilometres (350 miles) of reinforced soil levees encircling the city to stop flooding. There is a system of pumps to clear water from the city following heavy rains but the flood control was inadequate for coping with major storms. Just prior to Hurricane Katrina, a study was being carried out to see how the levees could be upgraded. After Katrina, the United States budgeted to spend $14 billion (£8.55 billion) on Louisiana flood defences.

After the flood

The New Orleans government does not simply want to make stronger and higher levees that can cope with rare high storm events. It is working with water management experts from the Netherlands to take a new approach. This involves leaving green spaces and creating lakes to absorb floodwater, and developing wetlands and barrier islands in the Mississippi delta to slow storm surge.

It also involves rebuilding parts of New Orleans with housing that can cope with flooding. For example, the Make It Right Foundation is developing a district of low-cost homes on stilts, with space underneath for cars, to rehouse some of those who were forced to evacuate from New Orleans during the flooding.

Two newly constructed homes in a "Make It Right" housing complex in New Orleans' Lower 9th Ward. This is an area where many homes were destroyed following Hurricane Katrina.

"The system we have now in South Louisiana … is unsustainable. It is literally a patch-and-pray system."
Senator Mary Landrieu, speaking about the levee system in 2009, Louisiana, USA

LESSONS LEARNED

Towns and cities are growing far faster than rural settlements. Between 2000 and 2015, it is expected that urban areas will grow by one billion but rural areas by just 125 million. As we have seen throughout this book, growing urban populations are having immense impacts on the ways cities grow, and the areas where they grow (such as at coasts). Urbanization is creating congestion and transport pollution, reducing clean water availability, and increasing waste problems. It is putting pressure on infrastructure, which can make poverty worse for city dwellers with inadequate sanitation and housing, and governments' abilities to provide for their people.

However, the cities of the world are vital economically and offer great potential for individuals in terms of jobs and opportunities. How can we make sure that the urban poor benefit from economic opportunities? How can we balance the need for growth with preventing overpopulation and overuse of resources so that the environment is preserved for generations to come?

Curitiba, Brazil, won the Globe Sustainable City Award in 2010 for creating a strong and healthy community, through using innovation and promoting cultural, economic, and social development while ensuring future sustainability.

Sustainable urbanization

Here are some of the various aims (and solutions) we have encountered through this book to make towns and cities more sustainable:

• To plan city layouts that reduce the need for urban transport; have less strict zoning, and involve engagement between governments, businesses, communities, and individuals to create places where people want to live and work.

• To enforce and encourage building regulations and designs for low-energy- and low-water-use homes and other urban buildings.

• To regenerate historic buildings, slum areas, and brownfield land to help keep city centres in use and vibrant, and prevent urban sprawl spreading.

• To manage city traffic by providing good public transport, allowing fewer polluting vehicles, and designing infrastructure that encourages walking and cycling.

• To maintain and expand green spaces, both in and outside cities – not only to improve urban life, but also to reduce floods, and to retain or to supply water.

• To increase energy efficiency and use renewable energy sources to help reduce greenhouse gas emissions in cities.

• To reduce and manage waste through careful disposal, recycling, and reuse in order to lower environmental impacts and maximize the value of resources.

• To promote cheap, sustainable technology for urban areas that can benefit the vast numbers of people in less developed countries – not just high-tech solutions for the rich.

Making a difference

Architects worldwide are making plans for sustainable cities. But turning designs and concepts into reality is an enormous challenge for the world. It will require great commitment and difficult economic choices for governments and individuals.

Reducing your own personal energy use, recycling more, and using public transport in cities are all small ways you can make a difference as an urban dweller. And you can always put pressure on your local community or government representatives to be more sustainable – for example, by campaigning for cleaner air in cities, or for more sustainable transport. Reducing the environmental impact of cities in the future depends on actions such as these.

TIMELINE

c.3000 BC The first recorded landfill sites are created in the Cretan capital, Knossos. Waste is placed in large pits and covered with soil at various levels.

c.2600 BC Heyday of Ur, the world's first city, in Mesopotamia (now Iraq).

c.2000 BC Composting and recycling of bronze are common in China.

c.700 BC Settlement begins that will later become the city of Rome.

AD 27 Rome becomes the first city with one million inhabitants.

AD 43 London is founded by the Romans.

1408 Medieval German cities require the wagons that bring produce into the city to carry out waste into the countryside.

1588 Queen Elizabeth I grants special privileges for the collection of waste rags for papermaking.

1624 New Amsterdam is founded, later renamed New York City.

1666 Christopher Wren makes a new urban plan for London after the Great Fire of London.

1857 Frederick Law Olmsted and Calvert Vaux's design is chosen for New York City's Central Park.

1889 Camillo Sitte publishes *City Planning According to Artistic Principles*, advocating curved or irregular streets for ever-changing vistas.

1889 Soap manufacturer William Lever begins building Port Sunlight, near Liverpool, as a new town for his workers.

1898 Ebenezer Howard's Garden City model of town planning is published in *Garden Cities of Tomorrow*.

1900 London population reaches 6.5 million, the largest in the world at that time.

1903 Letchworth, the United Kingdom's first garden city, is developed and Hershey new town is established in the United States.

1906 Construction of the world's first motorways begins in New York City, USA.

1923 Country Club Plaza, the first car-oriented shopping centre, opens in Kansas City, USA.

1931 Empire State Building opens in New York City. This is the world's tallest building for the next 41 years.

1950 New York City is first city worldwide ever to have population of over 10 million people.

1955 The first international air pollution conference is held following deadly smog episodes in London (1952–1956), New York City (1953), and Los Angeles (1954).

1956 Southdale Shopping Centre, the first climate-controlled shopping centre, opens near Minneapolis, USA.

1957 Scientists at Scripps Institute in the United States notice increasing build-up of carbon dioxide in the atmosphere.

1960 The first Clean Water Act passes through the US Congress.

1962 *Silent Spring* by Rachel Carson is published, sparking a debate about the relationships between people and nature and leading to a ban in the pesticide DDT.

1970 US Environmental Protection Agency is established.

1971 Friends of the Earth launches its first campaign by returning thousands of bottles to the Schweppes drinks company in the United Kingdom, bringing waste and product disposability to public attention.

1972 Bottle Recycling Bill passes in Oregon, USA.

1973 Arab oil embargo reduces oil supply to the United States and oil prices rise in Europe. This spurs research into renewable energy alternatives.

1977 The first bottle banks appear in the United Kingdom.

1988 Scientists publicize the link between global warming and sea-level rise and increasing storm severity.

1990 UN report on climate change recommends reducing carbon dioxide emissions worldwide.

1992 UN Earth Summit in Rio de Janeiro, Brazil, agrees targets for carbon dioxide emissions reduction and creates an action plan for sustainable development.

1998 The warmest year ever recorded on Earth. Nine of the ten warmest years occurred from 1990 to 2001.

1999 Earth's population exceeds 6 billion. Half are living in cities.

2001 UN Habitat Report on global cities is published.

2005 Hurricane Katrina causes catastrophic flooding when flood defences fail in New Orleans.

Hammarby Sjöstad, a sustainable settlement is first established near Stockholm in Sweden.

2006 Population of Tokyo in Japan reaches over 35 million.

2008 Construction of Masdar eco-city begins in Abu Dhabi in the United Arab Emirates.

2010 The Burj Khalifa skyscraper opens in Dubai and is officially the world's tallest building at 829.84 metres (2,723 feet) high.

GLOSSARY

aggregate hard pieces of bulk material, ranging from sand to crushed stone or concrete used in construction

biodiversity variety of types of plants, animals, and other living things in a place

brownfield area of urban land previously used for industry cleared for redevelopment

carbon footprint measure of environmental impact of services or production of goods based on the amount of carbon dioxide they are responsible for

climate change shift in weather patterns, frequency of extreme weather events, and average temperatures caused by global warming

congestion when roads are crowded with vehicles, slowing the movement of traffic

corridor narrow strip linking two different areas (for example, urban and rural green spaces)

decompose break down or be destroyed by chemical processes, often as a result of the presence of living things, including bacteria

diarrhoea illness when faeces turn liquid, are produced more often than normal, and can cause dangerous loss of water and nutrients for sick people

emission production and release of gas

e-waste thrown away electronic appliances such as computers, mobile phones, and televisions

fossil fuel naturally occurring fuel, usually found below ground or under the seabed, that takes millions of years to form. Coal, crude oil, and natural gas are the three major fossil fuels.

global warming gradual rise in Earth's average temperature caused by increase in greenhouse gases in the atmosphere

green space open, maintained space such as a park dominated by plants such as trees

greenhouse gas gas that stores heat in the atmosphere. Carbon dioxide and methane are examples of greenhouse gases.

greywater waste water that can be reused without purification (for example, water from showers that can be used for flushing toilets)

habitat place where particular living things normally live

incinerator machine that burns waste at high temperatures

Industrial Revolution period in the 18th and 19th centuries when there was increased use of machines and rapid industrial development

industrial zone region of a settlement where businesses and industries are concentrated

infrastructure range of structures, services, and facilities organized by government for its people

landfill site area of land where waste is buried in pits under soil

less economically developed country one of the poorer countries of the world, including the countries of Africa, Asia (except for Japan), Latin America, and the Caribbean

levee embankment built to prevent flooding

methane a gas that is the main element in natural gas and is given off by rotting plants and manure

more economically developed country one of the richer countries of the world, including those in Europe, North America, and Australia

public transport system of trams, buses, and trains used for large numbers of people to move through and across urban areas

redevelop change an urban area by creating new roads, buildings, services, and businesses

renewable energy source of energy such as the Sun, wind, ocean movement, or wood that is replaced naturally or by people and therefore will not run out

residential area region of a settlement with a high concentration of homes

resin sticky substance produced by some trees that is sometimes used to bind other substances together

sanitation technology and systems used to keep people healthy, especially providing clean water and removing waste

sea-level rise increase in the average height of the sea or ocean

settlement place where people live and work

sewage used water and other human waste, usually removed from buildings in more economically developed countries

slum area of a city with poor housing and unplanned development

smog yellowish air pollution caused by reaction of gases in vehicle exhausts and from factories with sunlight

storm surge powerful push of waves of seawater on to land caused by high winds during storms

sustainable does not use up too many natural resources or pollute the environment

United Nations (UN) worldwide organization that promotes international peace, security, and cooperation

urban sprawl spread of city buildings into the surrounding countryside

urbanization growth of number and size of towns and cities

waste-to-energy systems that burn or decompose waste to release useful heat energy, for example for warming buildings

zoning restricting types of buildings or activities to particular parts of towns or cities

FIND OUT MORE

Books

Buildings of the Future (Eco-Action), Angela Royston (Heinemann, 2008)
Cities (Geography Detective Investigates), Jen Green (Wayland, 2009)
Planning for a Sustainable Future, Helen Belmont (Franklin Watts, 2007)
Renewable Energy Sources (Sci-Hi), Andrew Solway (Raintree, 2010)

Websites

View the interactive timeline and map showing changes in rural and urban populations and the global spread of large cities:
news.bbc.co.uk/1/shared/spl/hi/world/06/urbanisation/html/urbanisation.stm

An interactive tour around the Dharavi slum in Mumbai and interviews with people who live and work there:
news.bbc.co.uk/1/shared/spl/hi/world/06/dharavi_slum/html/dharavi_slum_intro.stm

Find out more about urban farming: **www.sustainweb.org/cityharvest**

Try creating your own city for fun! **kids.tate.org.uk/games/my-imaginary-city**

How do people create and change communities? Discover a little more about urban planning: **www.planning.org/kidsandcommunity**

The title of tallest skyscraper has changed hands many times through history. Look at the changing designs of skyscrapers in more economically developed countries using an interactive timeline:
www.skyscraper.org/TALLEST_TOWERS/tallest.htm

Discover more about sustainable cities by looking at the case studies on this website. You can explore the site by category – such as waste, energy, or transport – to learn about the initiatives being taken worldwide to use resources in cities more responsibly: **sustainablecities.dk**

The website "Cities of Today, Cities of Tomorrow" is a rich resource with lots of information about cities, urban expansion, the consequences of urbanization, and sustainable cities: **www.un.org/cyberschoolbus/habitat/toc.asp**

Visit this website to find activities such as quizzes and instructions on how to plan your ideal city: **www.un.org/cyberschoolbus/habitat/index.asp**

Topics to investigate

Polluter Pays Principle

Countries, regions, and settlements are increasingly using the Polluter Pays Principle (PPP). This is an environmental approach that involves determining the cost of clearing up pollution, finding out who caused it, and demanding that they pay the price of cleaning it up. For example, from 2012, Australia's Clean Energy Act will force the worst polluters in the country to pay a tax on carbon dioxide (or equivalent) emissions. People opposing the move say it will make companies cut jobs and increase the price of power to get their money back. Research the internet to find out some examples of where cities have used the PPP to force urban polluters to sort out the mess they cause.

A green future?

Can you imagine helping to design or plan the sustainable cities of the future? To do this, you will need training. Many people hoping to follow architecture degrees study maths, physics, art, or graphics. Architects face many years of training before they design actual buildings. Those looking to be planners often study geography, history, and biology. Using a search engine, look for information about green architecture or sustainable urban planning to discover more about what these careers involve, and case studies of days in the lives of real architects or planners. A good place to start is www.rtpi.org.uk/education_and_careers/planning_as_a_career.

Extreme weather

In November 2011, the International Panel on Climate Change produced a report predicting heavier rainfall, more severe storms, and droughts in the decades to come as a result of global warming. Coastal cities will be under greater threat because the extreme weather may intensify the impacts of rising sea levels. Create a map, using atlases or downloaded templates, and with information from books and your search engine, locating the most vulnerable large cities. You should determine population, rate of growth, whether major industries would be affected by extreme weather, and how sea-level rise would affect economic productivity.

Infrastructure time bomb

In many more developed countries, road and bridge networks, water and sewage pipes, and some areas of urban housing were built many decades in the past when populations were smaller. As a result, today they are inadequate and may be crumbling or rusting away. For example, in a 2011 report, the Urban Land Institute calculated that the United States would need to invest $2 trillion to rebuild and expand its overloaded and crumbling transport network. In less developed countries, infrastructure is often poor quality and not built to last.

INDEX